THE BLESSED JOURNEY

(part 1)

The love of humanity

BESSORA NEEMA HIRWA

pencil

ISBN 978-93-5667-014-3
© BESSORA NEEMA HIRWA 2022
Published in India 2022 by Pencil

A brand of

One Point Six Technologies Pvt. Ltd.
123, Building J2, Shram Seva Premises,
Wadala Truck Terminal, Wadala (E)
Mumbai 400037, Maharashtra, INDIA
E connect@thepencilapp.com
W www.thepencilapp.com

Author biography

I am very thankful to www.inkitt.com that helped me to start this book. Iam also thankful to my family and friends who helped me to proceed.

God bless everyone who takes his/her time to read this book. This book is written based on my own ideas.

CONTENTS

THE ARRIVAL OF BRONEY IN HAPPINESS

My name is Broney! I was in a good and happy family, everything I needed was near me as they worked hard for me to learn. I studied in a good school, I made many friends. They thought that I am from a rich family, but they didn't understand how much I did hard. they thought that I was like a city boy. But that was not true. At home, I had to work in other to survive.

When you make new things or good things, when you have used your skills well, many people think that you are from a healthier family. You can't understand how much we need to become riches. We always wish to get money, whether you can be with 10000000$ or not. You need more.
I was studying in s2 going to s3. While in grand-vacancy, I heard something bad from my siblings.

I felt very shy to be there. My grand-brother was saying that I am useless and more. He called me a dog and other animal names. I felt very useless. I had always to judge myself why all that was happening to me.

In life, it is normal, but not good while by your family. When you become worse to your family it can cause faults to your future. No reason to disagree with your family. Instead, you can leave. But before leaving, you have to ask yourself why, where, and when. So that your leaving could not be bored by anything.

But to me, I ignored that, not even remembering the whole years that I spent with my family happy and together. None I told about my leaving, I felt that none was useful at that time.

I just only prayed to God to understand my wishes of being Good and rich. It was not a good idea for me to leave and it was not a good idea to stay as there could become family conflicts due to my character.

Sometimes people do not understand who you are and why you are there! But ignore it because only God knows you better. Nothing could make me concentrate as I have already adopted myself not at home. I had nowhere to go as none of my family knew my plan. None could believe that such small things were boring me.
Some would think that I can accept how I lived but to me it was impossible.

I would not understand anyone, that's the reason why

I had not to advise them. Sometimes we think that only we are right but just understand what others think of us. They either think you are harmful because you fight, etc. But to me why did I was being treated like that?

I did not like to go away from home, I studied hard to win and more. I searched everywhere to gain profit. You cant imagine. I was a sinner but I believed to change. Now no full information on why I was being hated. I was very stressed.

I chose to leave, but I had nothing to eat, to drink, no smartphone or airtime just only 500fr and my school bag with few clothes and uniform. I left my home with my mobile and reached Cyunuzi after 30 minutes as I was walking on foot.

I took a tarmac road and started walking on the road Rusumo-Nyabugogo but not sure about where I was going.

It was about 8:27 pm when I reached Ngoma. I bought airtime but none to call and slept on the road. I set an alarm for 4:30 am. I slept thinking of how others were happy, I was feeling now how good is to ignore some family problems to survive. I was hungry and thirsty.

None to call, no enough money, no food. It was just problems. I could now feel how easy life is. I kept telling myself stories of heroism and terrorists, army and famous, etc. Until I was ready to sleep.

At 4:30 am the phone rang and it was my time to wake up. I woke up and continued.

I was very tired but kept up. Everyone would see how I was very tired and hungry. I was very shy so I was not able to beg. I kept on thinking of how many kilometers are remaining to reach Kigali. This annoyed me.

I was not sure that I will reach somewhere in town to buy juice and bread in the 400fr remained.I reached Rwamagana hall at 00:12 am. It was in town but every shop was closed and not able to buy the juice. Police officers and soldiers were passing near me and I felt secure to sleep. I was very tired and again slept near MTN Agent's hall, I set an alarm and slept.

It was about 8:30 am when I woke up, what shame? I felt shy as people were looking at a street boy, but nothing I had to do just to continue.

I bought a 200fr juice and a 200fr bread and ate. It is not a good thing for a youth to leave their home. Your family is supporting you even in your mistakes because they love you. Now I continued." Why are they parking near me? Who are them?" I ask myself.

It was a BMW car parking near me. The man in come out and he said" looking tired! Can we pick you?" " is it me you are talking to you?" " yeah!" He replied. It was good I had not to disagree. There was a woman in the car. " "looking good! What's your name? Where are you going and why are you hungry?" She asked

I replied," my name is Broney!, I am going to Kigali, I am hungry because I got a journey without transport and no money!" We conversed I told them why I am being leaving home and was immediately shocked. The woman asked the man whether they can carry me to their house as they had one child and were not able to give birth again. The man agreed and parked alongside us to buy something for us to eat.

I was adopted by their family. " hi my daughter! Prepare yourself and the house we are having a visitor" the woman said on the phone. The man immediately come and we ate as we were entering Kigali city. In a short time, we reached the Gasabo district as they lived near the convention center.

We reached a good new house. It was new and amazing for me to enter. The gate is opening slowly as we drove near it. The gate fully opened. What a strange thing! A miracle! My eyes would be blind at it! What was that? Continue reading with the next chapter.

THE JESSY'S SMILE MADE BRONEY MAD

" Hello, mum! you come early than I thought" the girl said. She was a beautiful girl that I hadn't Imagined meeting and becoming her friend.

I felt very concerned about whether she had a boyfriend but it was not true because I had enough time to talk with her, the man replied" don't worry my daughter. we always seek what is good for you all!" even though they were talking the girl was still looking at me.

the man immediately introduced me to her" he is Broney! your new brother."

"he will act like your brother and will be with you!" the woman said.

also, I was just looking at the girl. we come out of the car and entered the room. we started a chat.

she told me that she is Jessy." I am Jessy! my mum and my father introduced you to me!" I reply" sure! looking good like you don't work anything!"

" all who don't work look cute?" she asks. " no, but you are different. you see how hard are others hand! but touch yours, very smooth" I answered.

we continued she told me how their family lived, her life from childhood until now. " anyway, How old are you?" she ask. " Is it necessary to tell you my age?" I ask her.

"yeah for sure! we have to know each other as we are going to be together. don't you understand? me I am 15" she says. " okay, 15 too" I reply.

the girl was now very happy, smiling every time. I saw it and decided to start my ordinary doggy chats." you Jessy, have you ever kissed anyone?".

the girl was terrified but later opened her mouth to say. Instead of understanding, I was looking at her well-organized whitey tooth. " no" she says.

I did not answer as I have not understood!. " broney? have you understood what I said? I said " no" she repeated.

"then, did you ever wish to do that?" I ask her. and she answers " no".

I ask her" then why do you like smiling for showing boys that your face is nice!" " Who told you that it was my intention of smiling? it is just my hubby to smile!" she says.

I reply to her" are you sure, let us omit that ". she asks " anyway, you wanted to kiss me that is why you just focused on my lips! why had you not looking instead at my legs?" I answer" what can you get from legs?" " movement, me I sit rolling my body.

why had you not seen it?" she asked. " ah! no. just be serious and stop smiling"I tell her. she kept smiling, I also kept watching just her smile as I had been very excited with her lips. but I kept telling her to stop because I was being furious.

" Now I am laughing, do you know why I am laughing?" she asks. " it is because you want to show me your teeth" I reply to her.

"hhhhhh, you Broney! don't you see that my father has been hearing you saying that things?"

" What! were you here sir?" I ask him. He replies " yes I was, but nothing to be afraid of'. " had you understood,wwwwww what I was saying," I ask. " yeah" he replies. I ask him" example of what you understood", and he reply," you told Jessy that she smiles for boys to see that her face is nice!".

I felt terrible, afraid that maybe he was sad. he kept just smiling. I was very tired and needed to sleep. I was wondering to ask her for a shower but needed to first get water.

I took a shower at my bedroom door and went to find what. I bath. After some time I fell asleep. After 3 hours, the whole family was waiting for me in the room to talk. ' did that man tell my story to the lady?' I ask myself.

I kept being confident and come into the room. The girl was chatting and her parents were just looking at me. Now it is time to see read our conversations.

MAN: Hey Broney! You wake. Lady: He is looking nice.JESSY: Hey! Come and sit with me. Don't you even tell it yourself?MAN: What do you mean?

JESSY: Broney must always be on my side.

I was just looking at a good sit. I kept thinking, I wanted to sit with her but thought that her family would warn me at last time. Jessy was cute but did not know how to use signs to tell me something, she just speaks. I was not able to disagree with her.

Me: okay! No problem I was just thinking about why you are all here.Lady: we are just needed to understand you well. You know that we have not even told your parents. Man: we do not know whether your family will agree.

Me: why do they can't? Are they who brought me here....or it's me myself? No reason to wonder.
Jessy: you have to do that professionally and properly. I can't imagine myself without Broney.

Jessy now had expressed all her feelings to me about her family. They could now understand how much she liked me. The family continued and ensured that we will visit my family on Sunday.

Lady: okay, we will visit them on Sunday.Jessy: good news Broney! The computer and smartphone on the table are yours.

Broney: really! I was very interested in using them.

It was good as now I would be ready to do all my online activities. This family started attracting my heart.

The next day, it was Friday. They bought many enough clothes for me and Jessy. You can't imagine how expensive they were. They sent 120,000fr on my mobile money and the same to Jessy's mobile money.

The next day, Saturday we prepared all that we shall need on the journey. she says " hey Broney, remember that we must not separate while we will be at your home!" " no needy for that Jessy!" I reply to her.

it was a good idea to visit my family, I prepared gifts for my grandmother. the girl would help me. at noon Saturday, Jessy wanted to present me to her friends. she took my hand and goes out. we walked along the street.

the first knock was on a beautiful house. I can't imagine that that friend was my classmate. Jessy says " hello, cline. his name is broney! my new bo-- my new friend." I hugged her and become dumb, not able to say anything as at school they knew me as a patient and coward. I had nothing to do just to keep quiet.

Jessy" Aaah. Broney, you see. Cline will be your friend because she is my friend.

Cline: when have you been together with this boy? aah, not necessary, I am just inviting you to the Friday singers' concert. we will enjoy it.

it was not a good idea to keep quiet but was necessary. I lost something to do and I took out my headphones and connected them to my phone.

we turned back home. we ate, watching Tv. " hey Broney, why did you set headphones to your phone and you didn't want to hear our conversation with Cline?" Jessy ask me. I reply" she is my classmate, I had not to say anything as ....". Jessy asks" did anything harmful would happen that time?" " none but, at school, they find me as I am afraid of girls. she would laugh at me." Jessy requests me to just feel confident while I am with her. " I will be your guardian, none will harm you while I am with you Bro!"
I kept eating and watching the Tv. the man immediately come into the eating room. he says" hey

Broney! let me believe that you enjoyed your journey. we ate but talked and watched Tv. after eating I bathe and come again to the room to watch movies.

the girl come and sat together, she asked me what kind of movies I like to see. I told her about horror movies. we started watching DRUG ME TO HELL. she was scared. as the granny was appearing, she was hiding her eyes. "hhhhhhhhhhhhhhhhhhhhhhhhhhhhh" in movies. it was a scary scene, she immediately grabbed me and hid in my hands.

© CanStockPhoto.com

after the movies we took dinner, and later I goes to bed.

I was chatting with my friends. Jessy immediately comes in.

she closed. what does she want at night? is it allowed for opposite-sex children to sleep together? Does she for disturbing me? or she is there for love? please read the next chapter to understand.

BRONEY AND JESSY'S LOVE STORY

Jessy closed the door and come near my bed. she sat on. she kept silent until I said. " what is the matter Jessy?". "I want to talk with you!." she says. I reply"Okay, go on!" ." I am very cold, let me enter your bed cover, then I will tell you that thing." she says.

I kept silent, but then said yes. she come on my Bed cover. she asks" what do you think will happen tomorrow?' . "we will visit my family, Is that what you come to ask me? why didn't you type a message?"

"don't you want me?" she asks. " That is not true but coming here also is not a good idea, it is also bad! or maybe you want to use the computer, it is there, goes and take it. I want to sleep!" I answers. she ask" who told you that I want the computer? you are showing me that you don't want me. That I am nothing to you!"

"no" I reply.

she kept asking me many questions. I woke up and told her that we can go into the room for talking. the bed room is not a conversation room

she came. " you know Jessy!" I say. she comes closer ."now you can go to sleep, I just wanted to see that you can understand me even in good times!" she says. I immediately go to sleep.

the girl would not sleep because she did not achieve her intention. she took her phone and typed to me. she typed" Dear Broney, I am thanking the lord because you are here with me, I had not imagined meeting a guy like you. From now on, I wished to be your girlfriend, your lover, your guardian. Can you please accept?"

I kept silent thinking on it, vegetables eat children as Rwandan proverbs says. I was not able to type again because of joys. she called me. but I did not respond because of shame. I loved her, but I was not able to tell her it." what shall I do?" I ask myself.

she called again and I accepted." Broney, what's wrong with you? why don't you reply to my message?" she says. I reply " I am still thinking about it, maybe I will tell you the answer next time!". she asks" no dear, you know that tomorrow we will visit your family, we have to act like lovers! Could it not be good?".

" you know, we are still young, this is not the right time to be in love, you can't love someone you don't know!" I reply. she says" Don't ignore baby, you know me. I know you. Tomorrow is the right time to see your family. what else could be remaining? it is just your acceptance! I know that you also love me, but I need your confirmation."

" Who told you that I love you?". I ask her. she started singing Knowless's song: cause the way to look at me, cause the way you talk to me Biragutamaza... Ukukuntu ubundeba, ukukuntu umvugisha Biragutamaza.....

" but I just see you as my friend. We do not hate to see cute girls, but not always we love them!" I tell her. "Do you mean that you don't love me?" "ahhhhhhhhh! Don't understand wrong, please! who told you that all beautiful girls or handsome boys marry?" I reply.

she continues singing: Tobora umbwire icyushaka, Tobora umbwire ukubyumva ahari nakumva, winigwa n'ijambo, Mbwira......" " okay, I love you very serious, I was not sure that you loves me but now I understand!" I says. she replies" I was kidding Bro, I can't love you. Not every handsome boy gets cute girlfriends like me!" she immediately hangs up.

I cried enough, I thought that she loved me, but I was wrong. The whole night I did not sleep. I kept thinking of how she begged me. I judged myself. I said that I will not talk to her again. in the morning about 3:30 am, a message from her come to me. what was it?
Dear friends, it is not a good thing to Brag to someone close to you. be a friend of all people. that night I found out how bad is to ignore someone's request while I could achive it.

not only people can judge you from mistakes, but even your heart can also judge you. during the night I learned that Bragging sometimes terrifies others. we damage their feelings about us.

not only that I learned in that night, but I also learned to keep on going, never give up. you can ask yourself How I learned it? I woke up at that time to see the message. I was very curious about the message.

after reading I retained my joys, I remembered her daily smiles, I remembered her bedroom visit that night, I remembered how she introduced me to Cline, I started typing a Reply. Can you imagine the message?

it was written like this: my dear friend Broney, I understand why you said that lately, I understand how much you loves me because your conversations, your characters represent love in your heart. I am asking forgiveness because I made your heart sad, I killed your feelings, but now I am here to resurrect them, I LOVE YOU!

You cant imagine how I become, I felt like I cant live without her. Love is good when you get it a true love, but when bragging it end up in tears.
in the morning we wake, we brush, we take breakfast. no word from me and non word from her. we all kept silent until we finished eating. "Broney, why are you not talking about the journey we have today?" the man said.
i was not able to say because of the girl. I was still looking at her smile, fresh drinking, how she take the

cake, how she eats, etc. I started keeping smiling of nothing. now I got back my mind.

I explained how all will be going on during our visit. I told them a special time to reach home, we called my dad, my uncle& aunt, we called my grandmother. we told them about our visit.

It was at noon after lunch we departured from Kigali, we reached Kajevuba and we continued to Ntarabana-Kiyanza-Kiyanza, we parked the car. many peoples were looking at it. they wanted to see who come from it. but we stayed in until my dad come to greet us.

immediately, the man and the lady come out first to greet my dad." hello mister and miss!" my dad says.they talked few things. after them, we followed, me and Jessy. " Good afternoon dad?" I says. He reply" yes, Good afternoon!"

we talked about a few things, we greeted neighbors and we continued to the house. we Entered. things were well prepared. dad kept asking me a few quea stations, why I left home, how I am being treated. after his questions, I and Issy left the Conversation room and we goes out.

there we were talking with my sister who was still with dad. we chated.
SISTER: Broney, how was youweree: very well with this girl you see. Broney: Jessy, she is my sister! Jessy: hello! SISTER: hello! jessy, Jessye believe that you treat well Broney! Jessy: yeah, I do. how cant I treat well myyou boy friboyfriend
my sister immeditimmediatelytood that we are in love, she would not imagine that I loved a rich girl.

SISTER: Broney, anyway, you dont cadon'te, you dont evdon'treet your brothers and sisters, do you think that we dont midon'tou?, pleas just call us.
me: I had not to callhave you because it was a surprise.
we kept talking many thabout ings. the girl(jessy) Jessyme to show her all our vilof lage. I thinkedthought I told my sister to show her, but Jessy said that we all must go together. we goes togopa. we bought many things to give my grandmother that costed coste money me and Jessy had (120000+120000fr) we then carried them to the car.
we arrived at our grandmograndmother'siyanza-Burega-Butangampundu) at about 3:00 pm. we provided all that we have brought and entered a deep conversation with my old schoolmate. wherever I goes I was with jessy.
Jessyf my old friends knew that she was my girl frgirlfriendtook my number and hers. we come back at my Gtondmothers home. we chatted with my aunt and uncle. we left gifts for them. my dad was given a new motorcycle, my aunt was given my dads

modad'sycle.

we come back in the car and continued our journey back to kigali.

many days passed while we were in love. many of my web friends had already knew myknownlfriend. we attended the singerssinger's Fridayt. we were all together.

DATE

DATE

DATE

Long tiA longassed while in love with jessy. Jessyto go back to school come, I had to go to school. I wanted to study well and win my Examinations.

this caused a big problem for Jessy was very unhappy of loosaboutg me. She didn't wish with me, but she was afraid of where about I can GET a new girlfriend. She immediately requested her parents to replace her at the school I learned. this made me sad even though I thought of her. this would damage my studies. it was even in a bad time where when going to do NATIONAL EXAMINATIONS.

the parents replaced Jessy at the school I learned to. I started thinking that this will attract poor studying to me. I told her that at school we must realize the strength of our love, we must not show our classmaclassmatese love each other, I told her that we must just focus on our studies.

It is good to get a friend but not good when you make works of little mind. always have purpose and keep it up.

DATE

Tomorrow was now a time to back to school, they paid our school fees, they bought all we needed, we took our sim cards because phones were illegal in boarding schools, everyone took 50000 fr on his/her mobile money.

Every one of my classmates we was with during school time, Knew that I bring no Pocket money. But at this time, I had multiplied. This was strange and new to me.

It was time to go back to school, we left home, and her parents picked us up to schoup ol. she was registered and now it was her time to go to arrange her items.

Before she goes to the dormitory, we met Cline, she greeted her and she hugged me. we conversed a few things as now I have already been proud of my girlfriend.

she told me that we must meet before we go to the dormitory. what do you think would have happened to Broney and Jessy? please continue. Remember to find the next parties where Broney will forget jessy!